First Facts®

Christmas around the World

Christmas in GERMANY

by Jack Manning

raintree

a Capstone company — publishers for children

Raintree is an imprint of Capstone Global Library Limited, a company incorporated in England and Wales having its registered office at 264 Banbury Road, Oxford, OX2 7DY – Registered company number: 6695582

www.raintree.co.uk
myorders@raintree.co.uk

Brenda Haugen, editor; Gene Bentdahl, designer; Eric Gohl, media researcher; Jennifer Walker, production specialist

ISBN 978 1 4747 2572 9
20 19 18 17 16
10 9 8 7 6 5 4 3 2 1

British Library Cataloguing in Publication Data
A full catalogue record for this book is available from the British Library.

Acknowledgements
We would like to thank the following for permission to reproduce photographs: AP Photo: Bernd Kammerer, cover; Capstone Studio: Karon Dubke, 21; Corbis: dpa/Matthias Bein, 5; Newscom: Deutsch Presse Agentur/Stephan Jansen, 12, picture-alliance/dpa/Franziska Kraufmann, 18, picture-alliance/dpa/Hendrik Schmidt, 7, picture-alliance/dpa/Robert Schlesinger, 15, picture-alliance/dpa/Soeren Stache, 11, Westend61 GmbH/hsimages, 16; Shutterstock: Jan S., 8, LianeM, 1. Design elements: Shutterstock.

Every effort has been made to contact copyright holders of material reproduced in this book. Any omissions will be rectified in subsequent printings if notice is given to the publisher.

All the internet addresses (URLs) given in this book were valid at the time of going to press. However, due to the dynamic nature of the internet, some addresses may have changed, or sites may have changed or ceased to exist since publication. While the author and publisher regret any inconvenience this may cause readers, no responsibility for any such changes can be accepted by either the author or the publisher.

Made in China

CONTENTS

Christmas in Germany

Music fills the cold winter air. People hang lights on houses. The smells of sweet treats drift from homes. It must be Christmas in Germany!

Germans celebrate Christmas Day on 25 December. But they begin celebrating the Christmas season four weeks earlier. On 6 January the Christmas season ends. Germans call this day Three Kings' Day.

Germany

How to say it!

In Germany people say *"Fröhliche Weihnachten"*, which means "Merry Christmas".

The first Christmas

Christians celebrate the birth of Jesus at Christmas. Mary was Jesus' mother. Joseph was Mary's husband. Christians believe that long ago, Mary and Joseph travelled to the town of Bethlehem. The couple could not find a place to stay, so they spent the night in a stable. Jesus was born there.

Three kings saw a bright star that led them to the baby Jesus. The kings brought gifts for Jesus.

Christian person who follows a religion based on the teachings of Jesus. Christians believe that Jesus is the son of God.

Christmas celebrations

Many people celebrate Christmas at Christmas markets. There they listen to music and watch puppet shows and plays. Shoppers buy food, toys and decorations.

The Christmas tree is a big part of German celebrations. Parents spend Christmas Eve decorating the tree. When they hear a bell ring, the children come to see the decorated tree.

On Christmas Day many Germans go to church. They listen to the story of Jesus' birth. They also sing songs and listen to music.

Christmas symbols

Germans were the first people to have Christmas trees. Many stories tell how **evergreen** trees became Christmas symbols. One story says Germans believed evergreen trees and lights kept away bad **spirits**. Germans put candles on the trees to protect themselves from bad spirits.

evergreen tree or bush that has green leaves all year round
spirit ghost
clergyman reverend or priest who carries out religious work

Another story tells about a German **clergyman** called Martin Luther. He walked in a forest one Christmas Eve. He thought the evergreens and stars were beautiful. Luther cut down an evergreen and put candles on it. He thought the candlelight looked like stars.

CHRISTMAS FACT!

An Advent wreath is a circle of greenery with four candles. Germans light one candle the first week of Christmas. They light two candles the second week. They light three the third week. Finally they light all four candles the fourth week.

Christmas decorations

Christmas is a beautiful time in Germany. Strings of lights hang from houses, shops and lamp posts.

People decorate Christmas trees in many ways. Thin pieces of metal or paper called tinsel decorate many trees. Some people put candles, stars or angels on their trees.

Germans decorate their homes with Advent calendars. The calendar runs from 1 December to Christmas Day.

Santa Claus

Who is that man with the white beard, red robe and hat? Any German child can tell you that it is Saint Nicholas! Children leave their shoes out for Saint Nicholas on 5 December. The next day they find their shoes filled with toys and treats.

Some children write letters to the baby Jesus. They may ask for gifts. Some children put the letters on window sills.

CHRISTMAS FACT!

Some children believe in the *Weihnachtsmann*, which means "Christmas man". He looks like Saint Nicholas and brings gifts on Christmas Eve.

Christmas presents

Presents remind Germans of the three kings' gifts to baby Jesus. Family members give one another presents on Christmas Eve. Some families read about Jesus' birth before opening their presents.

Children may get dolls or trains. Some are given jewellery such as rings and necklaces. They may also receive clothes, books or games.

Christmas food

German homes are filled with wonderful smells at Christmas. Families eat many different foods during the Christmas season. Some eat roast goose or roast pork. Others eat turkey or duck. A fish called carp is another popular Christmas food.

Gingerbread is a popular Christmas treat in Germany. Some people use gingerbread as decorations. They make gingerbread biscuits shaped like stars or bells. They hang the biscuits on Christmas trees.

Gingerbread houses are popular too. Germans decorate the houses with icing and sweets.

CHRISTMAS FACT!

Marzipan is a popular Christmas treat. It is made from ground almonds, egg whites and sugar.

Christmas songs

Have you ever heard the song "Oh Christmas Tree"? What about "Silent Night, Holy Night"? Or "Hark! The Herald Angels Sing"? All of these songs were written by Germans.

Christmas carolling is popular in Germany. Many years ago, poor people went from house to house. They sang outside each house. Sometimes the singers were given small gifts. Many Germans still enjoy Christmas carolling.

CHRISTMAS FACT!

Many German town bands play songs during the Christmas season. Bands play music in town squares. They also play songs in churches.

MAKE A CHRISTMAS TREE

The Christmas tree is an important symbol in Germany. You can grow your own little Christmas tree at home!

What you need

- one large pine cone
- one large bowl
- warm water
- one large plant pot
- soil
- grass seed
- scissors

What to do

1. Remove any stem from the pine cone. This will help the cone stand up.
2. Fill the bowl with warm water. Soak the pine cone in the water for 10 minutes.
3. Put 2.5 centimetres (1 inch) of water in the plant pot. Remove the pine cone from the bowl and put it in the pot.
4. Sprinkle soil onto the pine cone. Then sprinkle grass seed onto the pine cone. Put the pot in a sunny place.
5. Check your pine cone every day. Add water if the water level falls below 2.5 cm (1 inch).
6. Grass will grow on your pine cone. The pine cone will look like a Christmas tree. Trim the grass with a pair of scissors when it gets long.

GLOSSARY

Christian person who follows a religion based on the teachings of Jesus. Christians believe that Jesus is the son of God.

clergyman reverend or priest who carries out religious work

evergreen tree or bush that has green leaves all year round

spirit ghost

READ MORE

Big Book of Christmas Decorations to Cut, Fold and & Stick, Fiona Watt (Usborne Publishing Ltd, 2013)

Christmas (Holidays and Festivals), Nancy Dickmann (Raintee, 2011)

Germany: A Benjamin Blog and His Inquisitive Dog Guide (Country Guides), Anita Ganeri (Raintree, 2014)

WEBSITE

www.bbc.co.uk/languages/christmas/german/

Discover Christmas traditions in Germany!

INDEX